Composed

anthology of poetry
2024

Composed

anthology of poetry

2024

THREE OCEAN PRESS

Library and Archives Canada Cataloguing in Publication

Title: Composed : anthology of poetry 2024.
Other titles: Composed (2024)
Names: Rebrec, Angela, editor, author.
Description: Editor: Angela Rebrec.
Identifiers: Canadiana (print) 20240345592 | Canadiana (ebook) 20240345770 | ISBN 9781988915517
   (softcover) | ISBN 9781988915524 (EPUB)
Subjects: CSH: Canadian poetry (English)—21st century. | LCGFT: Poetry.
Classification: LCC PS8155.1 .C66 2024 | DDC C811/.608—dc23

Editor: Angela Rebrec
Copy editor: Kyle Hawke
Cover and Book Designers: Angela Rebrec & Kyle Hawke
Proofreader: PJ Perdue
Cover Image: *Untitled* ©2023, Corrie Clark

Three Ocean Press
8168 Riel Place
Vancouver, BC, V5S 4B3
778.321.0636
info@threeoceanpress.com
www.threeoceanpress.com

First publication, April 2024

To all the authors
who donated their poems for this anthology fundraiser

To the volunteers of past
UNBOUND Poetry Festivals

And to the volunteers of this year's
COMPOSED Festival of Poetry and Writing

Thank you.

ACKNOWLEDGEMENTS

"Aquarium" (© 2010 Fiona Tinwei Lam) was published in *The Best Canadian Poetry in English 2010,* ed. Lorna Crozier and reprinted in *The Best of the Best Canadian Poetry in English: Tenth Anniversary Edition 2017* (Tightrope Books, 2017).

"The Wild Absence of Time" (© 2023 Diana Hayes) appeared in *Sapphire and the Hollow Bone,* Ekstasis Editions 2023.

"Deerness" (© 2020 Al Rempel) was previously published in an Alfred Gustav chapbook under the same name.

"Portrait of a mother beside her children" (© 2023 Angela Rebrec) appeared in *Tenth Muse Literary Magazine,* Vol xiii, 2023.

"forecasts" (© 2014 Daniela Elza) was inspired by the poem "Angst" by Alexander Block (1880–1921). First published in *Ping Pong: An Art and Literary Journal of the Henry Miller Memorial Library* (Big Sur, California, 2014). It also contributed to the Watch Your Head Project: an online journal of creative works devoted to climate justice and the climate crisis from 2019–2023.

"Kootenay Glacier Crush" (© 2023 Anna Eastland) was featured on The Habit Podcast, Summer 2023.

"potential paths of a pebble" (© 2018 Kyle Hawke) was written and first performed as part of the Mashed Poetic Series, inspired by the song "Jonas and Ezekiel" from the Indigo Girls album *Rites of Passage.*

"What You Can't Take with You" (© 2015 Shirley Camia) appeared in *The Significance of Moths,* Turnstone Press, 2015.

 "Canoe—" (© 2023 Kate Marshall Flaherty) was first published in *Titch,* Piquant Press, 2023. Scan this QR code to access the performance video of "Canoe."

TABLE OF CONTENTS

FOREWORD

It brings me great pleasure to introduce our first anthology of poetry, a collection born from the generous contributions of participants from our previous two UNBOUND Poetry Festivals. This anthology represents not only a celebration of poetic expression, but also a testament to the spirit of poets coming together to support free literary programming to all who live in the Metro Vancouver area.

When a handful of us embarked two and a half years ago to establish the Delta Literary Arts Society, our mandate was ambitious yet clear: to provide diverse and enriching literary programming for free to all ages in all three of Delta's communities. The idea for this anthology arose as a fundraising endeavour to support the ongoing efforts of our society. The response from our past UNBOUND participants was overwhelming, with poets generously offering their work for inclusion in this volume in support of our rebranding as the COMPOSED Festival of Poetry and Writing.

As you delve into the pages of this anthology, I invite you to not only appreciate the beauty of the works within, but also, to reflect on the power of literature to unite and inspire. It is through projects such as this that we continue to nurture vibrant literary communities throughout Metro Vancouver, across Canada, and abroad, always with the goal of fostering the imaginations of readers and writers everywhere.

I extend my deepest gratitude to all who have contributed to the creation of this anthology — whether through their poetry, their support of our events, or their unwavering dedication to the literary arts. Together, we have truly made something special.

Angela Rebrec
President
Delta Literary Arts Society

JUDE NEALE

Grey hospital sheets and clouds of hate cover us

Love is the only salve
for spilled blood and

curses tossed
like Gretel's Bread.

Connect us through
desert and delta,

the saffron dust of Africa,

and in the blind eyes
of Michelangelo's David,

dove white—

they must be spared
from this unholy brutality.

The Amazon jungles
and chasms of deep

cenotes of sapphire, echo
back the guns aimed

at where we hide our pain.
The world is on the edge

And all I can see is her face, a ladder of tears.

Cynthia Sharp

Sleeping with Books

Inhaling the exhilarating
bouquet of new print
by the golden glow
of the reading lamp,
I taste little pieces of prose,
then fall all the way in,
comforted in the texture of pages,
soft as sun-warmed
Belinda's Dream roses,
inviting the inscription of
free verse rhythms
in the sleeve.

Highlighters and ink stars
bleed wild flowers
across aqua-coloured
Egyptian cotton sheets.
Water lilies blossom
in the sapphire satin blanket,
spirals of petals and sepals
arising like Northern Lights
over Greenland.

Sipping jasmine tea,
in bed with my books,
my soul unto itself,
I speak aloud
my deepest revelations
of passion and awe,
how much I love
the home they are to me.

Barbara Baydala

Once

I've come here from
the complacency of this morning and
yesterday afternoon. I remember
him from the very beginning. My
beginning not his. Mysterious in
black wool coat and defences. I don't
remember where I was. Somewhere
in the hallways with the first
two braless girls bouncing
ahead of me, imagining my mother's
horror. Imagining the walk home
safe in my parka my feet on
the usual path. Road on the
left, light reflecting off church
windows to the right. Baby sister
waiting at home. Imagine her
joy at seeing me. Starting from
that moment. Our futures our own.
Beyond the past and patterns of
what it meant to be a girl child
one of four or four billion.

Andriana Minou

The faulty dress

The woman's dress changes colour every time she enters
a different room. It turns yellow in the kitchen, red in the
bedroom, blue in the living room, white in the bathroom.
The woman's dress always matches the colour on the walls.
She tries going out in the garden and her dress turns green.
She calls the seamstress to complain. She bought this dress
to make an impression, but the dress seems to be faulty.
The seamstress apologizes, she promises to come and take a
look at it later tonight. The woman sits in an armchair, she
reads a fashion magazine to pass the time. All this ground-
breaking fashion puts her to sleep. Night falls and she's
still sound asleep, dreaming of herself walking in rooms,
making an impression. The seamstress walks in the living
room. She's looking for the woman, but it's so dark she can't
even see past the end of her nose. All she sees is a blackness
thicker than night itself.

Fiona Tinwei Lam

Aquarium

Delicate, unworldly
seahorses behind the coral.
The grey one holds high
its noble, elaborate head,
the white one, belly full of child,
drifts near. Their tails
entwine as hands,
even their unravelling
a slow caress. One hovers
while the other wanders
amid the anemones' waving tendrils.

Outside the glass,
my young son and I stand rapt
before this little paradise
as if it were a film
we must memorize
or perish.

His father has left us.
Probably for good.

Jeffrey Mackie

Moon in the Arctic Sky

Moon in the Arctic night sky
Flashes suddenly
Like a headlight on a celestial vehicle
Or the star hanging over the manger

There is no illumination
Besides the car lights
On this two-lane highway
Silence and beauty

Far from the world at war
Same world different war
Or perhaps the same as
When we were lovers in a dangerous time.

In this present time
I drive alone
In this ancient place
I am given time to ponder

The brilliant light
And where it shines
When it was the only light
In this forested landscape

You said
That you never cry in the darkness
Because the tears won't shine
To light the way forward

But out here
You would have to cry in the silence
If you wanted to be heard
If you wanted to be found.

DIANA HAYES

The Wild Absence of Time

Down by the tawny marshlands
a day like all the others lost
unseasonable and overcast
a third summer of pandemic's gloom

I sit for the longest while
listen to the swoosh and sway
of reed canary and leatherleaf sedges
watch purple martins flap and glide

their iridescent geometry
of feathers in flight
persuade me to break free
from this measured path

where questions lurk and breed
slip from six o'clock newsreels
hunt like no-see-ums
trailing me down to the marsh

I cast them away
like old winter socks
sink my feet down
in riparian soil

as sunlight's last ripple
drops through amber sky
then paints an indigo
so deep and clear

leaving me to breathe
the scent of dusk
this holy earth
the wild absence of time.

AL REMPEL

Deerness

farther down the road
where the lupins grow
in a big indigo patch
every summer in that field
I saw a small shape
go across tawny-brown
fox   I thought
about the right size
but when I got to the spot
slowed down
a small doe was staring
back at me
alert & still
making a space in the universe
deerness
let's call it
just as powerful
as the animal itself
my God palpable
even after I drove on
it stayed with me
then the rest of it
piled on
the farmhouse & trees I passed
you in the passenger seat
we are all pushing out
our essence
even rocks
into this malleable
infinite field
which is perhaps
what space is for
in the first place

SAMANTHA JADE KRILOW

This Intergenerational Jaw

biting
grinding
clenching
since time
immemorial

this pitbull maw

mauled
and mangled

jagged teeth
wrenched
from fresh
pink gum

i crunch
and spit
plastic

my torn
inner flesh

an iron grip
of anguish

jaw muscles
tightening
and twisting

around
this ancestral
strain

Tom Konyves

Channeling Gertrude

Everyone hears voices.

The voice I heard that night was the voice she used to write the names she used in writing:

"make a name for yourself"

what if the name makes the sound of a smoke alarm when it makes us listen up to the sound, it makes us rush toward the sound like a long lost one, one who has been lost to us without a sound, now there is a sound of one who may have been lost only to us, not without a name, but a name whose sound makes someone stand up and turn to us rushing toward them like a long lost someone whose name is the same

now what if the name is the same as someone else who has not been lost to us, but with us all the while and he or she is the same one whose face is so familiar that we would recognize them no matter where they were, he or she, and even if they came up behind us in a sudden wind whose touch was not immediately familiar but whose face was as familiar as could be

and if the sound of the name is recognized by someone who hears the name and suddenly the wind dies and the sound of the name is clear to us but not to someone who still hears the wind rushing to meet them at the train station

who has not recognized the sound of the name he or she hears at the train station, can the sound be recognized to make someone turn into the wind and still hear clearly, the name whose sound is the same as when they left and were lost to us who will always recognize the name and the sound of the wind rushing toward the train station

and the more we hear the sound of the name the more we begin to recognize that it is the same name we have always heard from a distance and it continued to sound in our ears as if we had always heard the name, no not a sudden wind, would make us turn toward the voice who said the name because it was familiar

or if it was so familiar that the name was the same as so many other names whose sound, like the wind in a train station, where the sound of names and places and time and faces are many, so many

now they say that you can't go home again because it is not the same home you left when you were lost to someone in a place and time we recognize when we hear someone speak about this or that place or time and it is always the past where it is all so familiar and even if it is not we don't have to be so careful about what we do

if the name is familiar and we recognize the sound as someone who has left us for far away where the past is unfamiliar and the sound is not one we recognize but one whose sound makes the sound of a whistle, we turn to face the direction of the sound and if he or she is different from the one who is lost to us, we turn and return to the home where he or she is sitting on the steps and smiling

Ingrid Rose

skull & cross::bones

close to sea's salty caress
under upper lip
remains of bones

         nouns   read   quick
                  said   quick
                  white under nail

                  quick::sand
people become bone
quarrelsome too
                  wrench yourselves
                  out of morass

                  in a sticky place no wonder
                  lack salt lack water
                  oxygenate   hydrate

                  once out on deck
                        walk the plank

black flag
at half-mast—

                  redeem us
                      pirates of this world

Luca Santamaria

Self-Indulgent *Transatlanticism* While the World Explodes

In the back of my car reciting lines — I turn and ask you to stay;
  we forget how your part went.
Something the curve of: "The tide's too high today." Dusk rattles
  the dashboard compartment.

It breaks loose like a black dog chasing a blue bird.
  The break-up is syllogized.
Its blood spatters on a red book I bought and hennas the
  cover — alters its core impartment.

I am, I am, iamb. The rhythm walks across the page
  with nowhere to go and
I'm writing goddamn, motherfucking conjunctions again —
  necromancing the Yore Department.

The sun drapes a plastic fox in scarlet strings while
  the garden-shed partition caves in —
they say grief's blue but blue's a dead-end. We were yellow & alone
  in a motel shore apartment.

A hundred academics scrape my refuse pile and
  Apollo comes down ticker-taped in revisions.
When the contemporary's buried & the ones we love along with it,
  they'll say "We get what your art meant."

MERRIDAWN DUCKLER

The Spectrum

The mood of the river is to glitter
which also is a way to deflect,

if I had to name its surface,
I'd say it was the colour of a sweaty disco tank.

Colour is how we comprehend the length of light
and what constitutes darkness is not without controversy;

water swallows all of the spectrum
except blue, which is what it reflects.

But this river is green. Like the nails on the airport attendant
who wanded me in a long-ago security drill

then bent close, sniffed my perfume
and said Opium, man that takes me back

and I won't say she exactly did the Hustle
but I won't say she was exactly still.

WINSTON LÊ

your lexicon made you do it

distort   wav file of recorded cochlean-hearsays   transmit
tile-transcription across ineffable scrabble turn despite twelve
word-score at hand your alpha-breath refuses to kinship-
connect f a t h er or word-wraith construct ba—what moves
are left across gridlocked board   you overhear transmissions
second language ghosts jibber-jab inside your auditory
cortex—

embody   code-mixed letterforms into viêtglish jabberwock
until this lexeme can   re-communion itself   becomes
Dia butchered freudian-synth of synonymous pronoun
Tía—misheard alveolar-morphism of d is mnemonic for
dad—crossword-cannibalize phantom semblance with what
spare language remains on your semantics-rack—

acquire   more malleability to carry over this haunting
   your fingers quest into velvet draw bag & sever linguistic
d & a/sunder apart from each other

disembowel   persona i orphaned in between   upon
that hollow square place   e for estrangement inside trigger
word's new coprolalia corpus   it always numbs you
banish it out of resonance chamber of your vocal folds—
d/e/ad

ANGEL-CLARE LINTON

what to do when you feel as if your poems are beginning to feel stale (not a comprehensive list)

1. Freak out a little on the inside.
Sometimes, when your mind
goes a million kilometres an hour, you think,
How can I improve my poems?
It can be good because the next thing you know,
you've come up with the next theme
of your collection and you pretend
you knew what you were doing
from the beginning as you have your fingers glide
over the keyboard. If
that doesn't happen,
you move on to step number 2.

2. Wonder what could have gone wrong and if you should continue your poetry career.
Sometimes, you wonder if
you shouldn't be "just" a poet. Sometimes,
there's a little part inside of you wondering
if your poems are good enough
to keep creating one collection after another.

Maybe if you feel "special" enough, write a poem
about how you feel as if you're not enough,
and you must continually breathe above water, screaming
as you fight for your survival
as if you're an animal that must be caged
"for its own good."

3. Begin planning a stand-alone novel and then the first book in a series and grow attached to both of them.
And then when you begin writing
as if you've been writing anything other

than poetry for most of your life, you realize that
the math ain't mathing, and you wonder
how to fix it, but you've failed
Math 8 and 10
and you've convinced yourself
since you were 13 or 14 years old
you're bad at math, so
you subconsciously think
you don't know how to solve it.

> **4. Realize that poetry is the medium for you
> while you still hold those novels in your back
> pocket just in case, one day, writing anything
> but a poetry collection is ever so slightly
> easier than when you tried 'x' amount of
> months or years ago.**

Realize that you've been blessed
with the ability to write   decent   poems
while you sit in whatever room
inside your house with a show
playing in the background
as a new poem sprints into your mind, desperate
for you to catch it.

> **5. Continue to write your emotions into
> poetry while you sit somewhere in your
> house as your fingers type away at the
> keyboard as if it's the only thing keeping
> you alive, and pretend that you aren't having
> a crisis about your poetry.**

Pretend
as if you knew what you were doing from the beginning,
and go back to pretending as if you weren't
comparing yourself to random strangers on the internet.

KAGAN GOH

Jonathan Livingston Seagull Finds a Girlfriend

My friend Nadia invites me to Steveston
Heritage Fishing Village in Richmond, BC.
I have been secretly wishing for a holiday,
and the Universe was obviously listening,
for Nadia answered my prayers.
Meeting Nadia was like meeting a fellow dodo bird.
She's an incurable romantic like me.
And now she's taking me to her favourite spot in the world.
She says, "There is a place I know on the outskirts of the imagination,
a vantage point on the edge of time
where we can watch the most spectacular sunsets."
How can I resist such a sumptuous invitation?

Nadia lends me a bag full of romance novels
to read to fuel my passion as I write my own take on the genre,
reinventing the Harlequin romance
as if written by Jack Kerouac, Henry Miller, and Pablo Neruda,
with a heavy dose of sex, spirituality,
shamanism, psychedelia, and disco to boot.
Nadia says romance novels are a form of escapism for her.
She believes in true love. She believes in happy endings,
where the princess marries the gallant knight in shining armour.
That is who I am, a knight in shining armour without a princess.
I am always in love. Take some. I have plenty to spare.
And deep inside I wish I had someone special
with whom I could share all this happiness.

At Steveston, families are having smoky barbecues.
Lovers stroll along the shore. Children play merrily.
"Next time we should fly some kites," says Nadia.
The evening is balmy. All my cares evaporate into thin air.
We walk through a field of purple irises,
speckled impressions like a Seurat painting.
I must get out into the countryside more often.

Soak up the greenery. Drink in the scenery.
Cool the fires of my urban city soul.

"Here we are," Nadia says.
A vast expanse of silver drapes over the sea like a veil.
A hazy sun hangs lazily over an azure wash of sky.
Pastel smears across the cheek of the sinking sun.
In the distance, a shimmering band of gold
where the sea meets the sky.
The islands are flanked by a panorama of lavender blue mountains.
The islands in the distance conjures the song
"Islands in the Stream" sung by Dolly Parton and Kenny Rogers.

Often, Nadia comes here alone and savours the sunsets,
not escaping *from* reality, like her romance novels,
but escaping *to* reality. I must remember to watch more sunsets.
A reminder of the vast expansive infinity of love's symphony.
Wooden poles stick out of the serene waters like exclamations.
Right ahead of us there are two seagulls perched on the same pole.
Their beaks touch and I swear they are kissing.
A Hallmark moment. A picture-postcard of sweetness.
Nadia chirps merrily, "Jonathan Livingston Seagull has found a girlfriend."
I laugh, but it's true. I'm glad Jonathan Livingston Seagull
has found a girlfriend and wonder, When will my time finally come?
I'm not looking for love. That doesn't work.
Neither am I shutting myself off. I'm open,
and if love flies in my window, I won't chase it away.

I shiver, it's getting cold. We decide to leave.
The light fades, but the image of Nadia's special place,
the vista at the end of time, shimmers like a mirage
forever burned into the retina of my mind's eye,
lingering like the melody of the ballad
of the rest of my living and undying days.

KEDRICK JAMES

The Composed Mind

"My vocabulary did this to me." —Jack Spicer's last words

How close can I hold you with these ginger fingers?
I am so still I might begin to decompose…

I gather resolve like a horizontal tarp at dawn
might half-fill a glass with water, each drop an intention
of, an initiation of, the suspended stone weight above.
This way, when the time comes, I might concentrate
my thirst into a moment of fluid song on my desiccated
tongue. That way, I might start to find my lost voice.
It squeaks like the metal wheels of an old tram I know
it's mine, my composed mind, finding me like mama
penguin knows her chick in a frozen colony where
earth empties its magnet into the southern astral sea
where chaos eats the ions of our brilliant mistakes.
I have seen the best intentions of my own generation
go awry, wandering with dementia, lost, forgotten,
until a hapless angel disguised as a gas station
clerk calls the number sewn into the neckline
of a fleece windbreaker that warms it barely
"we have your intention, please come and get it".

My composure is as flimsy as venal praise.
Of all the dissembling congregations of the Christian
Lost and Found, of all the diasporas of Galilee and
the gnostic dioramas underfoot, all the dispersals
of Alexandrian generals in the foothills of time itself
of all unresolved guilt of maternity ward settlers
none can be more misconstrued, deconstructed
or discombobulated than this final dedication
in light of the grounded theory of, this woeful
unbinding of, a mind poetry tried to compose.

Rose Renaud

Blessing from the Gods

Leave us by the ocean breeze of salt taffy affection, my love,
blessings from the gods flooding any faulting threat, my love.
Allow the permanence of spiraling galaxies to burst
lustre for lightyears of flourishing cobalt stars, my love.
May we walk among these cosmic and celestial beings who
bow for no one but each other's vault-filled mercy, my love.
Savour moments of our quiet outside of the chaotic world
for not all shared escapades exalt the same, my love.
The serenity of your companionship is what I lust for,
the gods forever forbid it all come to a halt, my love.
Our garden that has mapped our intimacy sprouts Roses,
its protective thorns burst from asphalt now gleaming, my love.

Angela Kenyon

Three days before you died

you asked how I was feeling
and all my words
fell
short
like when I try
to skim stones
across water

the angle
the pitch
the rhythm
of the syllables
only arc toward the telling
a stone's slip and sinking skid
sounds scattering like refracted light

write a poem, you said.

ANGELA REBREC

Portrait of a mother beside her children

> *After* Armenian Mother Mourning, *1919. Wikimedia*
> *Commons. Photo*

We will never
see her face
in that grave shadow
cast by the olive tree
to her left.
The gasp that pauses
at the edges of our mouths chokes
as a diminished
chord.
She sits in the ploughed field
beside swaddled chrysalids
positioned like markings
on a dial,
and behind,
the blurred image
of a man
walking away
from her
towards a grove.

Daniela Elza

forecasts

it is how our footsteps   alter   the flurries
how we move   through the breeze
                              in the boughs of our hope

when time stops   in the sideways glance
you will find me   in the missed heartbeat

see me   in the many moons of your longing
and furies.

            in the place where words   fail us

with a sharp   astute   parlance   and
war is upon us and   the sun sets black
                              under the yoke of

            a darkening century   again
we are going nowhere   fast.

                        in storms and   tornadoes
of prognosis and forecasts

            over a horizon of planted crosses
  the weather turns
                        passive-aggressive on us

and there is no way   we can say   such things
                              about the weather

as we forget how to move through   the elements
that   we are.

it is up to you and I   what we will do
            in this tortured   oil-spilled   winter

                    where   even in sleep
loneliness changes us   re-interprets us

                                                    holds us
hostage.

                    how   I even begin to smile at people
    in my dreams.

how a little bit of light brings nuance to the shutter—
in the long exposure photography of   grief

where the struggling light   shreds   the clouds of
  our sorrow   into the rags of tomorrow

and
of course

                    you will also find me here   waiting
                                                    for spring.

Lara Varesi

My Untangling

Along the way to purgatory my path veered,
and I found myself in a thicket of edged brambles
intertwined with contrition over long-past delusions
I have held of mending versions of myself.
Sharp and pointed memories slice into me
and all the false moves I have constructed
are unlocked and open.
There is nowhere to hide from them anymore.
They pour into my awareness with their suffocating
tentacles, grasping with attempts to drown me.
Bright and stinging, smarting.
I do not take heed.
I barge through, lacerating my skin,
hearing the mutilated past tear away from my bones,
not to be put back together, ever.
I set it free.

To begin the act of releasing old songs
that no longer need to play themselves out in my mind.
Their timbres dancing among the synapses.
Quickstepping to the rhythm of rumination.
Waltzing to the beat of "What if?"
I am weakened though, by these movements.
I wolf down a meal of crow that sticks in my throat
as I gaze upon my choices that have led me to this place.
Those that should probably be forgotten now.

I pretend they are only ethereal dreams that came and went.
Surreal and unreal to the truth of this moment in time.
A putative reality that fades away with each step taken,
as if it never really was.
As I traverse this new terrain, these thoughts still prod me,
following me.

Nagging like an uncomfortable and rough tag in my shirt,
rasping against my neck to remind me of its presence,
scratching at the membrane of the back of what is me.

With each step forward through the prickly, pronged path,
I feel each one shoot through my body like a sudden cramp.
One that seizes me with its acuteness, stops me in my tracks.
My progression halted, drawn backwards.
As I push this new birth out into my world,
breathing with the contractions of fear,
I am allowing this life to emerge without struggle.
To propel out of me as if thrust by a booster,
its strength enough to envelop me, become me.
To untangle me before I am put back together,
yet different now.

Anna Eastland

Kootenay Glacier Crush

Slipping into a hot bath
To escape my nasty cold,
I slip back in time
To that starlit night in the hot springs
Just after high school,
When I came home from the city to visit
Our village of New Denver.

You and I there in the woods
With a few friends,
Soaking in the heat
As the cool dark caressed our faces,
Upturned to see nothing but cedars and starlight.

My foot gently touched yours, just barely,
A quiet question, unanswered.
I drew in the crisp night air
And held my breath—
Wonder-drunk with the nearness of you.

And you, a gentleman in disguise,
The former class ruffian,
(Remember how you used to tease me at school?)
Now taking me out as a friend,
For old times' sake;
And I, aflutter with your kindness,
Sinking deep in the warm embrace
Of water and wondering "What if?"

After the hot springs,
We went to the local pub
Up the hill in Silverton.
You bought me my first glass of wine

And brought me home to my parents' doorstep,
Hugged me goodbye.
And that is all.

But all I could think about for months was you.

I finally got up the courage to send you a card,
Way back then when mail was more of a thing.
I remember it had a drawing of an old-fashioned car on it.
I don't remember, but likely
Some hesitant confession of love inside—

It went unanswered.

Years later, time having fled,
And you and I both married with children,
I heard the crushing news
Of the death of your son—
Only ten years old,
With big brown eyes like his father—
Drowned in the water at Christmas,
When your car crashed
Over the hairpin curve of the highway
And into Slocan Lake.

My chest tightened,
Hearing of your near-hypothermia
As you went back down again and again
Into those glacier-fed waters
To rescue him,
But could not.

Wild sorrow reawoke in my belly,
For I know the pain of losing a child—
My own little daughter died in my warm womb
On her way out;
She met the world in silence.

Both taken in the water,
By waters no longer safe,
Unlike the hot springs
On that summer night long ago,
With the night's coolness kissing our skin.

Now the slow weight of time
Has carved out our hearts like a glacier;
Sorrow's unstoppable scarring
Imprinted on the landscape of our lives.

I want to touch you again,
To find that boy from high school
And wipe away his manly tears
Or let them mingle with mine.

My desire is a silent prayer,
My heart reaching out to you
Over the many miles between us—
For now, I meet you only in memory.

Diana Calliou

Spring Rain

Fresh hits me as I step outside
Light rain, barely noticeable
On my face, I feel alive
The purple lilacs bloom around the corner
Catching wisps of fragrance
From the newly mown grass
And the pile of cedar mulch delivered yesterday
I imagine I smell the cedars ringing my yard
My body feels renewed, excited, determined
To live, to love, to care
To break, bow and weep for losses — mine and others —
In this rebirth season
Tears mingling with rain, heavier now
Constant rhythm, like my footsteps
Beating a path around my neighbourhood
Stranger sits dry in her car, planning her day,
Windshield wipers adding a new sound
To the cacophony of steps, rain,
Birds chirping, singing, twittering from the trees
Connecting living and dead
Love found and lost
Tears and rain.

KATE MARSHALL FLAHERTY

Canoe —

Carib word for dugout,
        Arawak for slender craft,
paddle-propelled,
        birch-bark or cedar,
   wooden ribs,
seated gunnels

slip of narrow boat
        through liquid,
lightweight, fish-shape—

keel-less vessel, we are
        in water, but not wet—

beneath the bay
shimmering shadows dart
and gather

a dragonfly alights

        our J-strokes smooth,
maple-wood paddles
        shellacked and shiny
in summer sun

dip and slide and swing—
little droplets in a line—

the rise of rock in the distance,
a scraggle of pine on the island

      … gulls and clouds dot the sky …

as we pull and glide in unison,
as we pull and glide in silence,
            the island in our sights

the V-trail from our stern settles,
            in our wake

KIM TRAINOR

Some notes on oldgrowth specklebelly lichen (*Pseudocyphellaria rainierensis*)— transcription and portal, tree licker, sparkling archive

Undulant lobes, *a pale greenish blue upper surface*, a
green algal photobiont, a cyanobacterial photobiont as
internal cephalodia, *ragged, lobulate to isidiate lobe*
margins, cryptic, found only at the yellow cedar drip zone,
in coastal rainforests of 300 years or more, a pale glow,
a pale lower surface bearing scattered small white spots
sparkling, poikilos, ποικίλος, in gloom.

16 September 2023. Foxtrot and I navigate a Forest Service
Road called Gordon Main to the 29th km marker. To what
remains of Savage Patch camp after the most recent RCMP
raid. Giant western screech owl made of salvaged wood, owl
guarding Eden Grove, tossed into a salmon-bearing stream.
Scattered flesh. How lives are destroyed.

poikilos, in gloom, tree licker, lichening to
a pale lower bearing scattered small
pseudocyphellae, soredia

There's a sparse crew at Savage Patch. We consult with the
matriarchs—Uncle Rico, Wee One, geegaagi. There's Big
Mouth, Donna and Bob too. Foxtrot and I do a supplies
run to Lake Cow, using Cook's hand-scrawled list—white
cabbage, coffee, peppers, black beans, black bean sauce,
salsa, hummus, cayenne pepper, bread, chow mein noodles,
potatoes, cheese. It's dusk at camp when we return and set
up our tents, sheltered by trees. Rig tarps for anticipated rain.
String fairy lights.

dull, naked, and pale greenish-bue
pale brownish, minutely hairy

greenish-blue, blue-listed
archetypal and synergistic

O Grandmother tree! O Grandfather Tree!
O greenish blue-listed oldgrowth specklebelly!
O lichen.

The kitchen is set up under a tarp, under the trees. There's a
jar of garlic scapes in water, a Coleman stove, bottles of olive
oil and hot sauce. Jars of spoons. Big Mouth has cooked up
a pot of Kraft Dinner and fried breakfast sausages to chop
in. I'm mixing margarine, oil, mashed garlic into a paste and
frying pieces of bread. This will go to the builders at Savage
Patch, who are planning something new.

It rains all night. The trees drink deeply.
The huckleberry, the sword fern, salal, wild blueberry.
The tiny mosses, the lichens, salmon berry, skunk cabbage.
(It has been so dry. Cedars turn rust and gold, moss scrapes,
rough to my fingertip. The river is dry.) Come rain.
Come rivers of mist. Come rain.

At the entry to TFL 46 we pass a blue and orange sign:

> HELP PROTECT B.C.'S FORESTS: IT IS ILLEGAL TO CUT,
> DAMAGE, OR DESTROY CROWN TIMBER WITHOUT
> PRIOR AUTHORIZATION…IF YOU SEE ANYONE
> INVOLVED IN ILLEGAL HARVESTING ACTIVITIES,
> PLEASE REPORT IT.

We drive kilometre after kilometre through clearcuts and piles
of slash.

Bluegreen algal cells entwined by hyphae—
greenish-blue filaments. Blue-listed lichen.
Poikilos. ποικίλος. Sparkling.
Uncle Rico comes to our tents at dusk the next day. Can you

pick up Cook in Youbou? Camp name Dragonfly. When you get service, send her this.

A handwritten note:

> *Uncle Rico said to text you and meet you at the first store in Youbou.*
> *What do we want?*

As we drive into Honeymoon Bay, a text comes in from Dragonfly.

> *tequila + lime*
> *tequila + lime*
> *tequila + lime*

And another, as we approach Youbou:

> *the fucking pigs just drove past*

A male elk appears, middle of the road, indifferent to our approach. Dragonfly finishes her cigarette and climbs into the car. *You know what I call the RCMP? Really Corrupt Mother Fucking Pigs. They know it. And they know that I know it. And I know that they know that I know it.*

(Now we enter the forest.)

You are here, as we enter.
You are here, small lichenous body.
Pseudocyphellaria rainierensis, tiny and scattered.
You are fungal and green algal, cyanobacterial.
Naked, pale greenish blue.
You are minutely hairy with tiny black dots,
      a body of swellings.
You breathe all around us, you are
      tree-dwelling.

You are spot tested with droplets of potassium hydroxide,
iodine.
Your metabolites fluoresce under UV light,
        turn bluish and yellow.
You sound chords teased from colours.
Gauge of human damage.
Absorb pollutants, isotopes, toxins.
Sip carbon dioxide and water from rivers of mist.
Spin complex sugars out of light.
Transcription of the world's glacial memory.
Scribbled notebook. Wild archive.
Comrade. Symbiont. Poet.
Pseudocyphellaria rainierensis.
Oldgrowth specklebelly.
Green portal, *ποικίλος*, fairy gauze, klecko klecko.

Kyle Hawke

potential paths of a pebble

everywhere between here and there
    fell many before us
everywhere between here and there
    lies potential before us
so we all need to watch our steps

sometimes when i walk
   — before my foot lands —
i wonder if it might be rejected
    by the earth beneath
      because yesterday
        i left that somewhat lesser
      because tomorrow
        is coming far too fast

i ponder the path of the smallest stone
      struck by my shoe
whether i've taken it from
        where it belonged
    or sent it to where it needs to be
    and if that was my right

after all, this is not my land
      because yesterday
      because tomorrow
        it was
        is
      and will be
        its own

that pebble kicked out of place
    could become a stumbling block
  felling the lead horse of a conquering army
        or a liberating one

that pebble kicked out of place
could become a building block
how it sits
what it touches
where it goes
may just tempt possibility
spark the imagination

because yesterday
showed us one path
because tomorrow
may not agree

maybe that stone will be moved again
maybe crunched to dust
maybe the impediment that
births a rivulet
shifts the course
of the tiniest stream
draws a new landscape

because yesterday
was not scrawled in
that stone
because tomorrow
may yet be

each step forward
must be taken with care
lest it lead us astray
lest it lead us backward

each path we carve
through our days
could bring others to harm
could bring others to our doorsteps

the echoes that we've effected
   will ripple through the future
      from the path of a pebble
      to the fall of the grandest stone
because yesterday remains
   the cause of tomorrow
   until we set a foot wrong
      or set it right

it makes no difference
   why our direction differed
   whether we were steered
      by prophecies or by bullets
outcomes ask not of intent

shifted dirt and kicked stones
   they tilt the planet
   they uncover bones
nothing is buried so deep
that it cannot be unearthed
because yesterday will always own us
because tomorrow might not want to

nothing is so out of reach
that it cannot be unearthed
because yesterday has always owned us
because tomorrow may yet want to

there are prophets interred
      in every graveyard
and graveyards inherent
      in every prophet
because yesterday
   and tomorrow
      do not belong to us.

SHIRLEY CAMIA

What You Can't Take with You

do you remember the reeds that closed in
before they opened up to a world engulfed
by the blues of the sky and sea

a world where men whose faces
cracked like roasted pig skin
sent out smoky circles
cut by children chasing chickens

flies swirled in a cyclone
as the gulls swooped in

do you remember

a world before the rains
before the petals fell

one by one

TARA AVERY

Proserpere

> *Go now, Persephone, to your dark-robed mother, go,*
> *and feel kindly in your heart towards me:*
> *be not so exceedingly cast down*
> —Homeric Hymn to Demeter

It is the waking time.

Ended, your long pomegranate sleep.

Your lover's bed empty,
while at your mother's side—
eyes still heavy, heart still heavy—
you watch the flowers bloom.
They are meant, you think, to be beautiful.

Drunk on scents of lilac and hyacinth
more potent than wine,
you grasp at memories, dreams.
You have already forgotten the timbre of his voice,
the colour of his eyes.

       And so, you wake.

It is the living time.

In your hair, roses. In your cheeks, roses.

Days stretch long under your mother's watchful eye.
Body supple with health and colour,
you are every day singing, dancing—
every day chaste kisses and honeyed dreams—

every day forgetting.

At night, though, at night and in your secret garden,
your deft fingers breed nightshade, belladonna, oleander;
gifts for a man you think—
you almost remember—
might like such things.

      And so, you live.

It is the sleeping time.

Days grow short. Tempers.

Your mother watches the darkness.
You watch her.
And when you slip your hand—
too cool, too pale—into hers,
you see a ghost reflected in her eyes.

Walking a path of marigolds, you leave.
Head high, eyes forward, your body already longing
for a bed of orchids; tangled limbs and tousled hair;
hands and heat and lips and lust.
You do not look back.

      And so, you sleep.

It is the waking time.

KIMBERLY LAWTON

A Bird

A poem should always rhyme
A bird should always sing
With such uneasiness of life
One should count on these two things

CONTRIBUTORS

TARA AVERY is a writer, editor, and coach. After graduating from UBC with a BFA in Theatre, Film, and Creative Writing, she spent many years living abroad — AKA collecting material for future writing. Tara believes words have the power to unite, entertain, and teach us. Mostly, she's just thrilled she's achieved her childhood dream of working with them for a living. www.taraavery.com

BARBARA BAYDALA is a poet living and writing in the village of Ladner, BC. She began writing after her father died of Alzheimer's disease in 2006. Five years later she unexpectedly found herself writing poetry. In 2013, she graduated from SFU's The Writer's Studio. Her work has appeared in *Emerge 2013*, *CV2*, *The Haro*, and in *Geist*, where she was the winner of the 11th Annual Literal Literary Postcard Story Contest. In addition to her involvement as a founding member of the Delta Literary Arts Society, Barbara is also an active member of the Delta Stageworks Theatre Society and President of the Delta Heritage Society, which has been preserving and celebrating the diverse history of Delta for more than fifty years. She lives with her husband and their longhaired dachshund, Dobson. She is currently finding joy and inspiration in time spent with her four-year-old granddaughter and her two-year-old grandson.

DIANA CALLIOU is a poet who embroiders emotion and imagery. Drawing inspiration from nature, personal reflections, and the complexities of life, Diana invites readers on a journey of introspection and discovery through the power of poetry. When not penning verses, Diana can be found exploring the wonders of the natural world or lost in the pages of a good mystery. She currently resides in South Surrey, finding solace and inspiration in the simple joys of everyday life.

SHIRLEY CAMIA is an award-winning Filipina-Canadian poet. She is the author of four collections of poetry: *Mercy* (Turnstone Press, 2019), a finalist at the High Plains Book Awards; *Children Shouldn't Use Knives* (At Bay Press, 2017), shortlisted for a ReLit Award and winner of the Manuela Dias Book Design and Illustration Award at the Manitoba Book Awards and an Honourable Mention at The

Alcuin Society Awards for Excellence in Book Design in Canada; the critically acclaimed *The Significance of Moths* (Turnstone Press, 2015); and *Calliope* (Libros Libertad, 2011). Shirley's work has been featured in publications such as *Wasafiri*, *The New Quarterly*, *CV2*, *The Ex-Puritan*, and *TAYO*, as well as anthologies such as *Endlessly Rocking* (Unbound Content, 2019) and *My Lot is a Sky* (Math Paper Press, 2018). www.shirleycamia.com

CORRIE CLARK is a commissioned artist, expressing herself through acrylic paintings. As a versatile creative writer, actor, and businessperson, she has enjoyed a remarkable career in the entertainment industry. Corrie's journey includes over forty film and television productions. Notably, she appeared in science fiction shows like *The Outer Limits* and played lead roles in various movies. Her most memorable contribution was in the 1994 version of the feature film *Little Women*. Corrie wrote animated episodes of *Addison* for the CBC. Her versatility shines as she also contributes to a series of children's books. She has worked at a talent agency, and in casting and wardrobe. Corrie holds a certificate in Writing for Television from SAIT, as well as a graduate certificate in Children's Entertainment and Media. Her writing collaborations with museums and cultural organizations allows her to innovate storytelling and bring history to new audiences. Corrie is a single mother of three amazing daughters and embodies resilience and creativity in all aspects of her life.

MERRIDAWN DUCKLER is a writer and visual artist from Oregon author of *Interstate* (dancing girl press), *Idiom* (Harbor Review), *Misspent Youth* (rinky dink press), and *Arrangement*, a collection of flash fiction forthcoming from Southern Most. She won the Beullah Rose Poetry Prize from *Smartish Pace*, the Flash Creative Nonfiction prize from *Invisible City* (judged by Heather Christle), the Elizabeth Sloane Tyler Memorial Award from Woven Tale Press (judged by Ann Beattie), the Drama Prize from Arts & Letters in Georgia. She is an associate editor at *Narrative* and the international philosophy journal *Evental Aesthetics*.

ANNA EASTLAND is a Canadian writer and mad-poet mom of nine, with another in Heaven. Anna believes in the transformative power of poetry in dealing with loss and helping rediscover that life is still beautiful. She has been sharing her work on her blog, *Just East of Crazy Land: Adventures in Parenting*, for over a decade. Anna is the author of *unexpected blossoming: a journey of grief and hope*, and co-author of *Beginner's Guide to Growing Baby: Tips to Help You Through All Four Trimesters*. She has contributed chapters to three anthologies, with several more in the works. She is librettist for The Laments Project by soprano Ai Horton, who transformed Anna's babyloss poem "Carry Me" into a song of lament accompanied by harp.

DANIELA ELZA's fourth poetry collection is *the broken boat* (2020). Her first chapbook *slow erosions* (2020) was written in active collaboration with poet Arlene Ang. In 2022 she placed second in the Ken Belford Poetry Prize for Social Justice. In 2023 she won first place in the Muriel's Journey Poetry Prize, was longlisted in the 2023 Vera Manuel Poetry Prize, and won the 2023 September Award for Awesomeness at *Arc Poetry Magazine*, judged by Susan Gillis. When Daniela is not writing, she works as a poetry editor, mentor, and creative writing instructor.

KATE MARSHALL FLAHERTY has published eight books of poetry, most recently *Titch* (Piquante Press, 2023) and *Digging* (Aeolus House, 2022). She has been published in journals such as *The Literary Review of Canada*, *American Academy of Poets*, *CV2*, *Vallum*, *Grain*, and *Trinity Review*. She writes spontaneous "Poems Of the Extraordinary Moment" (P.O.E.M.s) for charity and guides StillPoint Writing and Poetry Editing Circles online. See her performance poetry at: https://katemarshallflaherty.ca.

Originally from Singapore, **KAGAN GOH** is a Vancouver-based Chinese Canadian multidisciplinary artist: award-wining filmmaker, published author, spoken word poet, playwright, actor, mental health advocate, and activist. He was diagnosed with manic depression at the age of twenty-three, in 1993. Kagan is a well-known spoken word artist, essayist, and poet, a respected and established voice in Vancouver's literary community for over two decades. He has been invited to perform at readings, festivals, and on radio, and has published in numerous anthologies, periodicals, and magazines. He is a graduate of the prestigious Humber School for Writing program and holds a certificate in creative writing from Simon Fraser University's The Writer's Studio. Kagan was writer-in-residence at the Historic Joy Kogawa House in Vancouver, BC, from November 2014 to February 2015. In 2012, Select Books in Singapore published his poetic memoir, focused upon his relationship with his esteemed father, *Who Let in the Sky?* In Kagan Goh's follow-up memoir, *Surviving Samsara*, he recounts his struggles with manic depression, breaking the silence around mental illness. *Surviving Samsara* was shortlisted for the Singapore Literature Prize in 2022 in the creative nonfiction in English category.

KYLE HAWKE has been performing spoken word for over thirty years. Active with various literary non-profit groups, he founded the Bohemian Caress and Voice on Canvas interdisciplinary performance series. Kyle's poetry is juxtaposed with the art of Wade Edwards in their book, *whispers of humanity*. Currently, he is working on a graphic novel with artist James Picard. He lives in Vancouver, BC.

DIANA HAYES was born in Toronto and has lived on the east and west coasts of Canada. She has seven published poetry books, including her newly released *Sapphire and the Hollow Bone* (Ekstasis Editions, 2023), *Gold in the Shadow* (Rainbow Publishers, 2021), *Labyrinth of Green* (Plumleaf Press, 2019), and *This is the Moon's Work: New and Selected Poems* (Mother Tongue Publishing, 2011). A new chapbook, *Language of Light*, was published by House of Appleton in 2023. In 2019 she launched Raven Chapbooks and publishes small-edition poetry chapbooks by BC poets. Since 1981, she has lived on Salt Spring Island—the traditional and unceded territory of the Hul'q'umi'num' and SENĆOŦEN speaking people. www.dianahayes.ca

KEDRICK JAMES is a poet, musician, and Professor in the Department of Language and Literacy Education at the University of British Columbia. He is the founder of the PhoneMe project, a social multimedia app for place-based poetry, and Singling, an AI text sonification software that converts written text to non-phonetic sound and creates skim-reading possibilities for people with visual impairments. As an educator, his work on transmediation and glitch pedagogy, poetic inquiry and arts-based educational research, and English language arts education is internationally recognized. He has published three books, dozens of scholarly articles, as well as other media such as vinyl LPs, CDs, cassette tapes, broadcast videos, and his visual art has been featured in galleries around BC.

ANGELA KENYON is retired now from full-time work and is grateful for this time to explore the creative process through writing. She is a graduate of the SFU's The Writer's Studio. She is currently working on the final draft of a novel that she started at The Writer's Studio. In the last couple of years, she has spent a lot of time writing poetry to find a path through grief.

Born in Budapest and based in Montreal until 1983, **TOM KONYVES** is a writer, poet, curator, and videopoetry theorist. A graduate of Concordia University, he joined Montreal's first artist-run centre, *Vehicule Art*, where he was one of The Vehicule Poets, a 'group of seven' poets "who…produced some of Montreal's most original multimedia performances, collage texts, videopoems, literary magazines, and books." In 1978, he coined the term 'videopoetry' to describe his first interdisciplinary work, *Sympathies of War*, and is considered "one of the original pioneers of the form." In 2011, he published the groundbreaking *Videopoetry: A Manifesto*, a "definitive guide" which has garnered more than 30,000 views from 67 countries. Tom is the author of 6 books of poetry and a surrealist novella, and has produced numerous public poetry projects and a Manifesto for videopoetry. His most recent book of poems, *Perfect Answers to Silent Questions* (2015), continues a life-long involvement with the experimental forms of post-modern poetry. He lives in White Rock, BC.

SAMANTHA JADE KRILOW is a Métis writer and storyteller living in Surrey, BC. She is an alum of the Audible Indigenous Writers' Circle, and her writing has been featured in *Pulp Magazine*, *Spraypaint Magazine*, and *Literary Cultures Journal*.

FIONA TINWEI LAM has authored three poetry collections and a children's book. She edited *The Bright Well: Contemporary Canadian Poems about Facing Cancer* and co-edited two nonfiction anthologies, *Double Lives: Writing and Motherhood* and *Love Me True: Writers on the Ups, Downs, Ins and Outs of Marriage*. Her poems have been featured in Best Canadian Poetry 2010 and 2020 (as well as the 2017 Best of the Best anniversary edition). She has collaborated on award-winning poetry videos that have screened at festivals internationally. Shortlisted for the City of Vancouver Book Prize and other awards, her work appears in over 45 anthologies. She teaches at SFU Continuing Studies and is Vancouver's sixth poet laureate. www.fionalam.net

KIMBERLY LAWTON is an author of short stories, young adult fantasy, screenplays, and poetry. She has been long-listed by the BC Federation of Writers for her short story, "Anger". Over several years her work has been presented in front of sell-out crowds with the Delta Literary Arts Society during their Killer Verse stage production. In partnership with the City of Delta her work, *Suki's Reindeer Wish*, has been presented annually during the Christmas season.

WINSTON LÊ is a Vietnamese-Chinese poet and inter-disciplinary artist who resides in Langley, BC. His writing has been featured in *periodicities*, *Sparkling Tongue Press*, *Ekphrasis Magazine*, *pagefiftyone*, and *filling Station*. His poetic practice encompasses different modalities concerned with language acquisition, including receptive bilingualism, poetic dictation, speculative poetics, and asemic writing. His debut chapbook, *translanguaging*, was shortlisted for the 2018 Broken Pencil Zine Awards. *translanguaging* is now curated as part of the special collections at Colby College Libraries in Maine.

ANGEL-CLARE LINTON is a poet, writer, editor, and publisher. She is also the founder of *Spray Paint Magazine*.

JEFFREY MACKIE is an internationally published and translated poet living in Dawson City, Yukon, located on the traditional territory of the Tr'ondëk Hwëch'in First Nation.

ANDRIANA MINOU is a musician and writer based in London, UK. She has published 5 books in Greek with Strange Days Books, one of which has also been translated to Spanish. Her latest book in English, *The Fabulous Dead*, is available in English by Kernpunkt Press, while her work has been published in several literary journals, anthologies, and websites internationally. She often writes librettos and texts for performances and films that have been presented around the world. She is also a judge for Eyelands Book Awards and a founding member of Coocoolili, a surreal cabaret ensemble, frequently performing in London. You may find more about her work at her website www.andrianaminou.com.

JUDE NEALE has written twelve collections of poetry and is an opera singer, mentor, educator, workshop organizer and facilitator, mother, grandmother, and wife. Her book, *A Quiet Coming of Light*, was a finalist for the League of Canadian Poets Pat Lowther Award. Jude collaborates with artists from many disciplines, notably in the 2018 poetry collection *Cantata in Two Voices* with Bonnie Nish, in *Where We Stood* with visual artist Jane Kenyon, and with violist and composer, Thomas RL Beckman, to create the original soundtrack for *Where We Stood*. She continues to be widely published nationally and internationally and is currently leading several comprehensive poetry writing workshops for gifted aspiring authors, as well as collaborating on a print media project with visual artist Nicholas Jennings in her recently launched book, *Water Forgets Its Own Name*.

ANGELA REBREC lives and works on the unceded ancestral lands of the Kwantlen, Tsawwassen, Musqueam, and Stó:lō peoples. She is a multidisciplinary artist whose writing has appeared in magazines and anthologies across North America. Angela's poetry films have been recognized at the Barcelona International Film Festival, FilmmakerLife Awards, and Santa Barbara International Shortfest, among others. Her writing has been shortlisted for several awards and contests including *PRISM International*'s Nonfiction Contest. Angela's 2020 collaboration with composer Mickie Wadsworth for ART SONG LAB has been included in NewMusicShelf's *Anthology of New Music for Trans & Nonbinary Voices, vol.1*. She facilitates writing and expressive arts workshops for kids and adults of all age. Angela is the founding and current president of the Delta Literary Arts Society.

AL REMPEL's books of poetry are *Undiscovered Country*, *This Isn't the Apocalypse We Hoped For*, and *Understories*, along with a number of chapbooks. He has a new book forthcoming from Caitlin Press in 2025. His poems have also appeared in a variety of journals, anthologies, and videopoem collaborations that have been screened internationally. Some of Rempel's poems have been translated into Italian and Spanish. He can be found at www.alrempel.com.

ROSE RENAUD is a graduating Creative Writing student at Kwantlen Polytechnic University from Surrey, BC. She is a mixed Filipina Canadian writer and poet who writes about the ups and downs of life. She has been published in *pulpMAG* and has received the 2022 Billeh Nickerson award at KPU. Rose has read at the UNBOUND Poetry Festival with the Delta Literary Arts Society. When not writing, she is loving cats, working on her Etsy shop, or streaming herself playing videogames.

INGRID ROSE has lived on the traditional and unceded territory of the Coast Salish peoples longer than anywhere else. Born and raised in London, UK, where she taught and wrote; then in New York, USA; Waregem, Belgium; and Velannes, France. Writing and reading are Ingrid's closest companions. She has learned tons from the writers who participate in her Writing from the Body Class she created over ten years ago, as well as from submissions published and rejected. Ingrid plans to self-publish her mixed-genre memoir: *The Walk: twin brother and woman's journey.*

LUCA SANTAMARIA is a writer, bird-whisperer, leaf-lover, floral shirt enthusiast, and poet who lives on the unceded ancestral lands of the Kwantlen, Semiahmoo, Tsawwassen, Qayqayt, and Kwikwetlem nations. Luca currently serves as President of the Kwantlen Poetry Project and Vice President of the Kwantlen Polytechnic University's Creative Writing Guild. You can usually find Luca taking himself much too seriously in the marshes of your neighborhood bird sanctuary or frolicking in the woods like a satyr when he thinks no one is watching.

CYNTHIA SHARP was the WIN Poet Laureate and the City of Richmond's Writer in Residence, as well as being nominated for the Pushcart Prize. Her poetry, fiction, creative nonfiction, and reviews are in journals such as *CV2, Prism, untethered, The*

Pitkin Review, and *Toasted Cheese*, among others. Her drama has featured in many festivals on North American stages, including Killer Verse, Take Ten, SAW Gallery, and the Chincoteague Theatre. She's the author of *Ordinary Light*, a first-prize winner in the SCWES 2023 Book Awards, *Rainforest in Russet*, and *The Light Bearers in the Sand Dollar Graviton*, as well as the editor of *Poetic Portions*. She holds an MFA in creative writing.

KIM TRAINOR is the granddaughter of an Irish banjo player and a Polish faller who worked in logging camps around Port Alberni in the 1930s. Her earlier books are *Karyotype* (Brick Books, 2015), *Ledi* (Book*hug, 2018), shortlisted for the Raymond Souster award, and *A thin fire runs through me* (icehouse poetry/Goose Lane Editions, 2023). Her latest book is *A blueprint for survival* (Guernica Editions, 2024). She has won the Gustafson Prize, *The Malahat Review*'s Long Poem Prize, and *The Antigonish Review*'s Great Blue Heron Poetry Prize, and has been anthologized in *Best Canadian Poetry in English*, *Global Poetry Anthology*, and *Worth More Standing: Poets and Activists Pay Homage to Trees* (2022). Her poems have appeared in *Anthropocenes* (AHIP), *Ecocene*, ISLE, *Ecozon@*, *Dark Mountain* (UK), and *Fire Season I* and *II* (Vancouver). Her poetry films have screened at the Zebra Poetry Film Festival (Berlin) and at +the Institute [for experimental art] (Athens), as well as in Dublin and Seattle. She has twice led Writing Poetry in the Forest workshops for the Delta Literary Arts Society. Kim's current project is "walk quietly / ts'ekw'unshun kws qututhun," a guided walk at Hwlhits'um (Canoe Pass) in Delta, BC, featuring contributions from artists, scientists, and Hwlitsum and Cowichan knowledge holders.

LARA VARESI began her poetry journey in 2010 and has since read for and hosted many events, including Mashed Poetics, Word Whips, Poetic Justice, Twisted Poets, Poetry in the Park, and the Dominion Reading Series. In 2014 she became president of Burnaby Writers Society, and she also organizes and hosts their monthly reading series Spoken INK. Through that, Lara has been fortunate to meet many inspiring authors from all over Canada. Lara was previously published in an RCLAS anthology in 2014 and is honoured and delighted to be a part of this anthology.

The Delta Literary Arts Society

The Delta Literary Arts Society began with purpose: to promote literary arts throughout Delta and beyond. Fuelled with drive and ambition, DLAS hit the stage with Killer Verse, its first event, little more than two months after the creation of the society itself, a drive that continues today.

Along with support of its members and community partners, DLAS has strived to provide outstanding programming at minimal to no cost. Entertaining children and adults with the written word brought to life, DLAS has become a visible community force. DLAS is responsible for ensuring programming has been available at local arts centres, libraries, classrooms, community centres, and online to speak to a core and fundamentally human experience of storytelling.

Featuring the work of local and international artists, DLAS is committed to lifting voices. Where there is a story to be told, words to be written, or a voice to be heard, DLAS is there to wholeheartedly support the artist, recognizing and celebrating the truth that literary arts are part of the human experience. The poetry and prose of this and previous generations are what bind the world together.

Encouraging representation, self-expression, and sharing personal truths are cornerstones supporting the mandate of this society. We welcome you to join us at our various events, including Killer Verse, Suki's Reindeer Wish, InkWellTold, Writers' Circles, COMPOSED Festival of Poetry and Writing, COMPOSED Short Film Festival, Teen Poetry Slam, Annual Poetry Contest, and Authors' Readings.

All of this seems like a massive undertaking for a small society located at the mouth of the mighty Fraser River in British Columbia, Canada, but the Delta Literary Arts Society is, at its core, the little society with big dreams.

www.dlas.ca

www.ingramcontent.com/pod-product-compliance
Lightning Source LLC
Chambersburg PA
CBHW051645120626
46551CB00015B/2228